dancing
with
elephants

kalyn marie nicholson

Koze Publiidhing | Toronto

Publishing | Toronto
www.allthingskoze.com

ISBN: 978-1-9994151-3-6 (paperback)
ISBN: 978-1-9994151-4-3 (e-book)

To anyone who might need a safe place to land tonight
or a cozy corner to tuck yourself into this morning.

To all the elephants that used to fill the rooms with all the words
I didn't know how to say.

To all the hearts that filled the poems within these pages.

To the end of a rich and challenging story in a slowly closing era.

To the start of a new chapter in a magical new decade.

🌙

language

If people hear it, they'll keep reading.
And if they don't, they won't.
But if you hide your voice—
If you keep this side of you tucked away
she'll keep building up inside of you
until she's pouring from your eyes
or clenching in your fists.
She'll find a way into your dreams
and keep stealing your screams
in just the same way
she feels her truth choked.

So let her pour it all out of you
without worrying who's pages the words may reach.
Lace her words to your lips and
learn to speak in her tongue.
Write her story, trust the author.
Release the filter, uncloak relatability —
don't hide in the shadows of the daylight
for fear of what might happen
if you were to step into the sun.

Turn up your song,
move to the beat
and finally set free
        all those pretty words.

IF LOST, PLEASE RETURN TO:

YOURSELF.

That's precisely what this project did for me.

These last two years I captured my thoughts as I learned to grow more into myself. All of these poems and journal entries become a love story in so many more ways than one. Between the destinations reached, memories marked and moments of bliss so rich I thought I might truly be tasting ecstasy (Dad if you're reading this, I promise you I wasn't) I not only found, felt and filled hearts that I'll never forget but more than anything I found, filled and came home to my own.

To trace the outlines of finding so many new sides of life in such a linear way could never do the magic justice; because it wasn't just about the faces, places, passions and scenes that wrote the script of a once lonely city girl...
It was how dazzling it felt to dance in such dynamic displays of the Universe, shining bright and brilliant in what felt like a million little moments left for me to find.
An energy force so full that within its pockets I found pits within me that reached so deep, only the prettiest of words seemed worthy to fill these pages.
On the days where my skies seemed to linger in greys both happy and haunting, I discovered a love for gathering up such fleeting and fluttering feelings and zone in a tongue that felt both old and new until words began pouring into journal pages and phone screens from fingers coming undone.   All I ask is that you might go easy on a girls first attempt to mirror her thoughts into symmetry and know that there are sides of my life and of myself in this book I've never shared before.
(Earth to Dad again, only read the copy of the book I gave you and sorry in advance for the missing pages)

For every poem you read, know it to be an old page in my life.
Moments I wanted to capture in more layers than just one.
Words that I wanted to say or scream but never did or got the chance to.
They are truths that struck me with the weight of a million elephants, dancing on my chest and stealing the air in my lungs. I had to find a way to set their fears free - the biggest one being the fear of sharing such a deep and personal side of myself with the world.

In facing that deepest elephant, I found a voice that wanted some space to shake loose and take occupancy.
I don't expect these pages to move you in the ways of Walt Whitman or Maya Angelou, but instead just wish they might rest on your eyes and feed your soul a little more permission to step more fully into your own light.
To stand up, dance it off and set your own elephants free.

**SO COME DANCE WITH ME
AND ALL THE ELEPHANTS IN MY ROOM**

may your actions breathe
your language

and your choices mirror
your truth

so you can speak your
soul fluently.

table of
of
contents

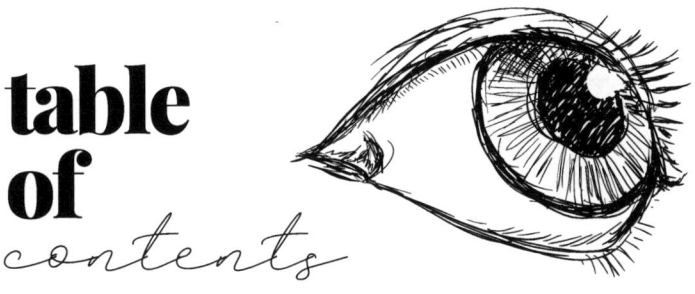

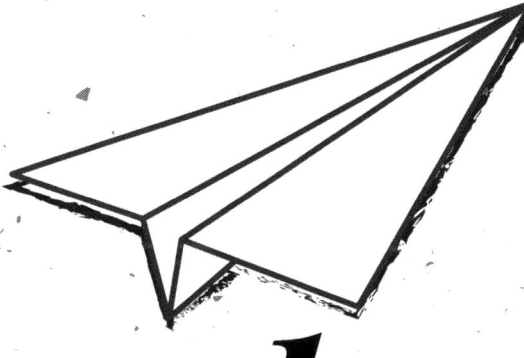

wander
lust

I longed to learn myself in places
I could leave behind a mark
only to find each destination
leaving larger marks on me

1.8.1

WE SURF THE CLOUDS
PLAYING COY TO THE JOY
OF WHAT IT IS TO FLY
INFINITELY FREE
WEIGHTLESS AND UNBOUND
TO THE WHOLE WIDE WORLD BELOW

I watched the mirrored moonlight
crack a match to winding rivers
bolting across each stream like lightning
striking and streaking the earth below;

igniting a fire in sleepless eyes
of new lands to sink my teeth into
& fresh air to breathe new life in;
lessons landing come daylight

two orders of french fries
and a bottle of chardonnay

you stole a piece of my west coast
as the sun faded over fireworks
sparking sunsets in July

and with atlantic Aprils
first of nevers that faded into
tangled viridity
me and you...
finding unfiltered truths

do you still think about it too?

YOU WERE MY
HALCYON PARADISE

maps pin paths to your location
crossing hearts like planes take sky;

chased away a best kept secret
found with you, new heights to fly;

drunk on love and dreams run endless
made our peace with short goodbyes;

but you knew this was hushed trouble
from the moment we caught eyes.

I want to run far from here
among a crowd to disappear
fall along forgotten faces
something new
a young girl chases

the cityscape afternoon

I dare my soul
a new adventure;
be yourself without the fight.

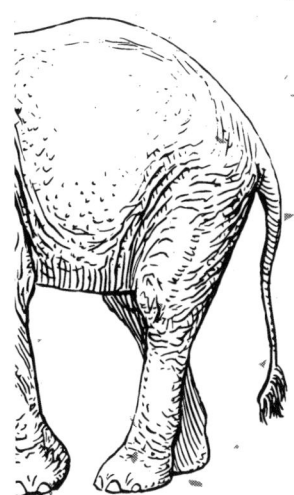

Dancing with elephants //

I chase the side of me that speaks
telling me to see the light;
the guide that said to grab my book,
unlace my thoughts and start to write.
to note the path of growing whole
as I put my heart to bed each night,
to follow flow, to feel a glow
& burn my fire its full bright.

pretty in pink
with fresh cut flowers
drinks tea in the afternoons
she rides her bike
and boys she likes
under light of the pink full moon

little lilac
late lavender sleeper
she eats breakfast at noon
loves starry skies
dulcet goodbyes
chases bad boys and good tunes

baby blue
a sea soft soul
always holds some space for you
floats in far clouds
swims in deep waves
can always teach a thing or two.

sunshine yellow
a solar life force
shines a light makes you feel true
dazed and dazzling
weightless and wild

...another place to paint her new.

**racing shadows
heartbeat drowns ears**

seat belt hearts buckle
salt seas seek new tears

the soft bones of a girl

in her calico dress

danced the jungle in circles

laid her head down to rest

soul weightless she waited

to fall life back in line

a quick race to the seaside

her heart healing each time

I tried to paint you grey

but love doesn't work that way

the desert sun hot
mind blazed on the thought
of what it would be like
to chase morning
                 in those arms

or if yours are the eyes
      I'll let sink into mine...
million things to be thinking;
but it's these thoughts that swirl a girl
on such a hot summer day

        want to come my way?

in seas of souls
with speakers bleeding
everything making me
slowly starts leaking

as I sway into the night
feet dangling; spirit float
I dance with the elephants
long caught in my throat

bass built in their stomping
rhythm wrapped in each spin
feel the movement prewritten
beat per word; infinite

20 something

do it all, chase the sky,
dont be afraid to fall and fly

1.32.1

Late Night Confessions

of my 20-something

intervention:

LOOK WITHIN

DON'T CHASE *THINGS*.
DON'T GRIP *TIME*.
IT ISN'T **YOURS TO** HAVE OR KEEP.

THE *MORE YOU RACE* IT
INSIST TO *CHASE* IT
THE *FASTER* YOU **WILL FEEL IT** *FLEE*.

FOLLOW **LOVE**.
CHASE *RESULTS*
THESE THING**S** ARE **YOURS**
WITHIN REACH
FOR WHEN YOU **F**ACE JT
YOU CAN TAS**TE** IT
TH**E** LIGHTER THA**T** YOUR SOUL WILL BE

I've always sort of felt like an old soul,
trapped in the teachings of how 'to be
young.

1990

1991

1992

1993

1994

1995

1996

city lights & busy streets
window panes & cool lined sheets
the souls you pass, the souls you meet
from stepping stones to blush red cheeks
known mistakes, unveiled deceits
question marks, new answers seeked
seasons pass like scrolling feeds
fun to run, play hide and seek
less excess & furtive greed
things this generation needs

KMN

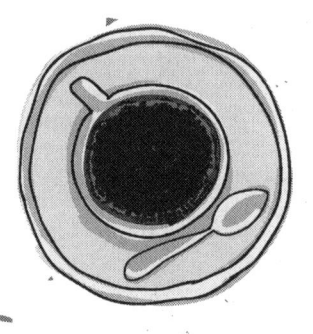

there will be days
you will find
your coffee hot
and your mood salty

know you are loved
just the same

*its nothing more than
a bad day.*

give me accents

& long nights

tall ones with

laughs light

quiet whispers

moon above

soft touch

gentle tugs

late walks

sleepy afternoons

give me all of it

do it all with you.

as long as you can feel your youth

you have it.

I just want to dance with you
at two a.m around my kitchen
swaying to the beat of another song
that writes a feeling we breathe life to.

I'll raise my arms above my head,
you'll tilt your head back in a daze;
twirling and spinning, eyes closed in the sweet bliss
of what it's like to be young and in love
tied to such a crazy world.

there will come a time

where you meet a

match you treat

differently than the

rest-

& in their light you

might dazzle but

always ask yourself

this:

do they see the light

that beams down on you too

do they treat you as warm

as you wanted them to

if the answer is no,

take power back in the truth;

just a marvelling muse

it's time you outgrew

if you don't change, you're too much of the same

but if you do, you're too something new

It's a cycle you see;

taking our broken hearts

& tucking them in the dark

of our far cornered closets

pulling our best dressed

up to the front

while we pop, effervescent

kissing reflections

refuelling our thunder;

& just as it roars

we open our drawers

& put our best player

back on the board

the time ticks on a clock
who's face looks just like you

as I lay in the darkness,
a sheer veil of vulnerability
lingering over all the ways
I wish to know you

yet the whole time I'm stuck wondering
who's eyes you may be looking into instead

let your hair down
rock a dark lip
show up in your most dazzling

life is short
so don't be afraid
to stand up tall

mind

if we close our eyes we see
everything thats meant to be
just focus in and breathe

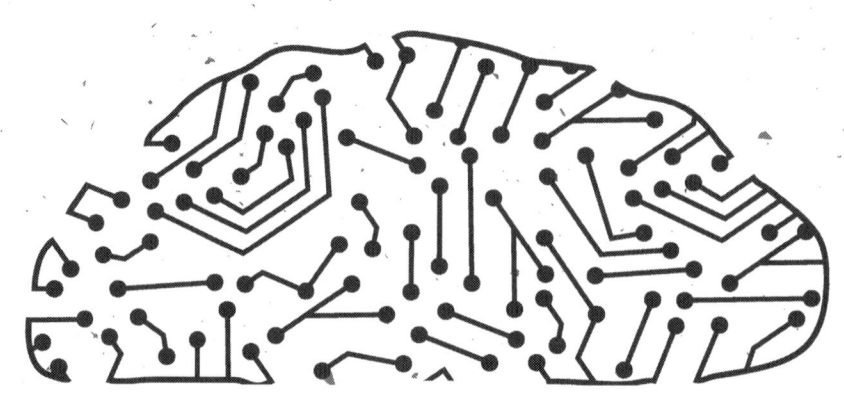

'DON'T TAKE IT TOO SERIOUS,
DON'T OVERTHINK TOO MUCH
LET YOUR MIND WANDER THE FILTER
THROUGH WHICH YOU SEE THE WORLD

YOUR AWARENESS, LET IT BE
A SAFE PLACE TO REST
A HEAVY HEAD
KNOW THE TRUTH THAT RESTS
OF NO NEED TO BE FIXED HERE

JUST A BUSY MIND FINDING TIME
FOR A LIFE TO BE LIVED.

Clouds call to me
in fear and distraction.
Ghostly sips on wines of worry
leaving me tipsy on solid ground...

I think it's time I put my feet back down.

I've often wondered what
it would be like
to be looking at the same skies
but through someone else's eyes

if even for a moment
locked within their time
instead of mine;

Who were they dreaming of?
Where to chase next?

to share in the light
of new perspective
with eyes to borrow
for I'm growing so tired
of seeing all these things
on my own

KMN

you're the worst distraction

for my already clouded mind.

I want to put my brain to work

but its your face that I find.

worst of all I tell myself

"just a means to an end"

but if that was so...

why do I find myself wishing that

all of my nights don't just start with you

but my mornings should too.

find your flow

weigh and measure
all this world brings
to a life recipe
of patterns so sweet
it warms the daylight
blues the skies
and frees your mind

pretty pictures flicker,
fluttering feelings of what life could be like...

and for a little while it's beautiful,
a scene I can't catch my minds eye from

but once in a while it might be nice
to leave there where it is
and just be here?

I was so stuck looking through the window

trying to see the bigger picture

that I was missing all the lessons

in the framework.

I've traced you in a million places
If solely written in my thoughts.

I'd seek new horizons but nevertheless,
wherever I went,
there you were.

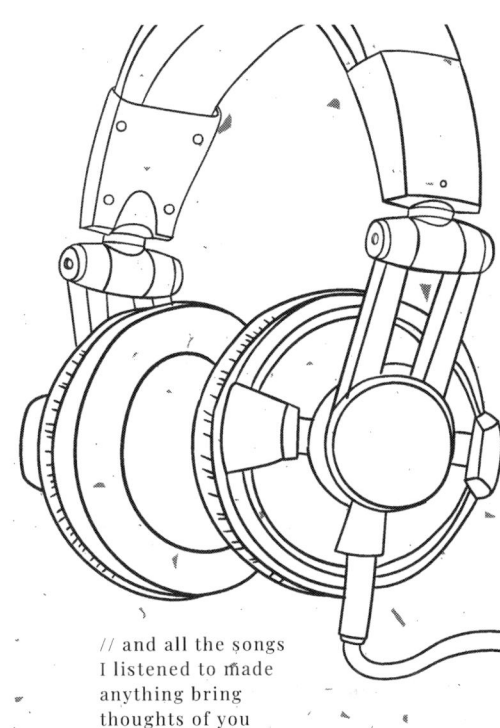

// and all the songs
I listened to made
anything bring
thoughts of you

You are as free as you find
your state of mind to be.

For unless your mind is
free, it is hard to truly be.

```
         I close my eyes
       to rush the skies
         elixirs of mind
           less and full


   float away in the offing
        of all that awaits
       unravel what's real
        to open the gates


          a ripple in time
        to sit in the stars
      ask jupiter questions
      burn fires with mars
```

KMN

body

from your first step to last breath
it blankets a soul with senses
to feel a life through
so treat it true

IF FRESH WATER FELL STRAIGHT FROM THE **SKY**

TO NOURISH AND **REPLENISH,**

WOULD SUNLIGHT BRIGHT AND FULL OF **LIGHT**

FREE OUR DISTRACTED **ANGUISH?**

IF SOULS WERE MADE OF **STARDUST**

& OUR BODIES GROWN FROM **GARDENS,**

WOULD WE THEN SEEK GOOD THINGS TO **EAT**

& POISONS THEN TO **PARDON?**

IF LIMBS WERE BUILT OF LEAVES AND **BRANCH**

& HEART BEATS RHYTHMIC **THUNDER,**

WOULD WE UNDERSTAND THE NEED FOR **RAIN**

TO BRING ANOTHER **SUMMER?**

IF LUNGS WERE WISPS OF CLEAN WHITE **CLOUDS**

& STOMACHS MARKED OUR **CENTRE,**

WOULD WE KEEP OUR AIR SWEET **ETHEREAL**

& TO OUR BODIES BECOME **LENDERS?**

Your body is your home.
It's the corners you think in,
the safe place you sleep in,
the one you take with you
                    wherever you go.

Let that be enough
to never let anything
crawl you out of your own skin.

They tell you to feel alive,
f i n d   y o u r   s e n s e s

but I say lose yourself to them.
Feel so deeply into life
that they all become one.

& as you melt into the world around you,
may you meet your flow.

YOUR BODY

is the vessel

between who you áre

& where you're going.

```
       blood electric
        palms on fire
          fatal taste
      of sweet desire

        eyes move slow
      like ocean tides
      hips meet heaven
        sacred bribes
```

slow down
sip me slowly
taste each note
until we float

soft hands
sink into me
no rush for places
know we'll go

breathe deep
layers changing
you soak me up
I drink that grin

s l o w   d o w n
so I can show you
all the shades
I see you in

KMN

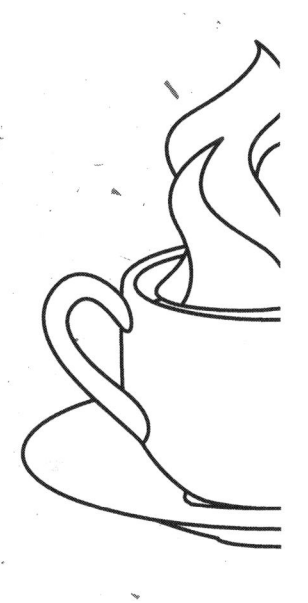

And just like the beat of another song,

weaving and waving its way through your bones –

does life become new again.

we lose our way
we cross our lips
we find our sway
waistlines and hips

I hope you kiss a thousand lifetimes

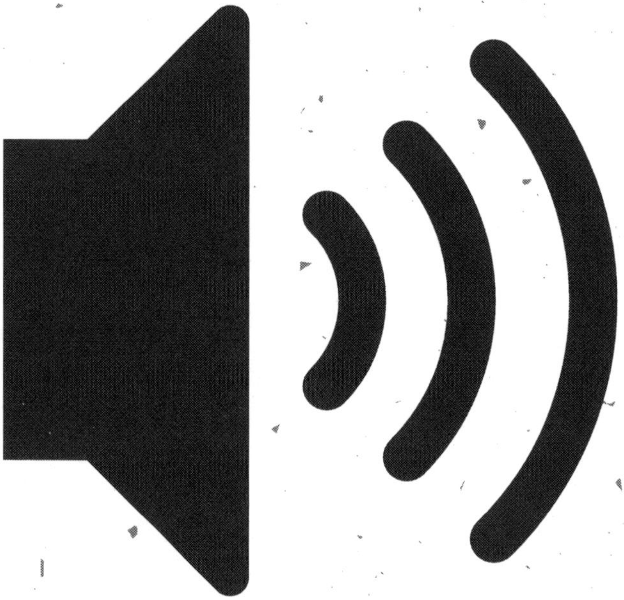

hitting pavement
killing kilometers
clouds like vapour
blood stained cheeks

eyes find skylines
faceless strangers
passing souls
places to be

race the city
my own pace
drown my lungs
so I can breathe

soul

an endless well of wisdom
a quiescent state of being
radiating within

I FEEL A NEW LIGHTNESS

CARRY MY BONES

PIXIE DUST IN MY EYES

GOLDEN GLOW IN MY SOUL

AN AURA THAT FILLS ME

LIGHT I CAN CONTROL

I SEE IT WITH FULL EYES,

LOVE IT WITH A HEART FULL

Everyday I wake in wait of what's coming

And forget to see what has already arrived.

maybe we were meant
to break things
just to learn how to put them back
together

character and novelty building with
every break and crack
until our walls crumble
and we set ourselves free

KMN

sweep away all beyond the blinding brain

where night then breaks a heavy fog

clearing cliffs that I fall

sullen and relentless

until my gossamer guides appear

ego fades, I float away

        their messages left clear

sleeping
they float
over the whole world below

insane becomes plain
unsound echoed loud
two souls fetch the free

hand in hand
learned and unlearned
their wrongs painted right

they wake themselves
through the chemistry
of bare hearts
& ephemeral endings

locking the wrists of the girl
& the breath of the boy
to a forever that would never be

your soul light like vapour,
laced with liquid lies
drunk on the heat
burning our forest fires
we danced on our kingdoms
fluid moves
bodies glide
took me in every moment
let me lift your sad eyes

hearts marked
constellations
passing souls
through these skies

one wish left
to ask of you
meet me in my next life

KMN

Lean into yourself.

Trust your intuition

She knows you better than anyone else.

It's a beautiful thing;
to feel so deeply, intensely, intently.
Not all souls can bare that depth.
Not many hearts can unveil that vulnerability.

Because to feel what it is to love at such great
depths means you agree to meet its maker in pain.

But you'll see...
the hurt you were placed here to feel is the
doorway to the love you were sent here to find.

For yourself,
For another,
For this life.
For the world.

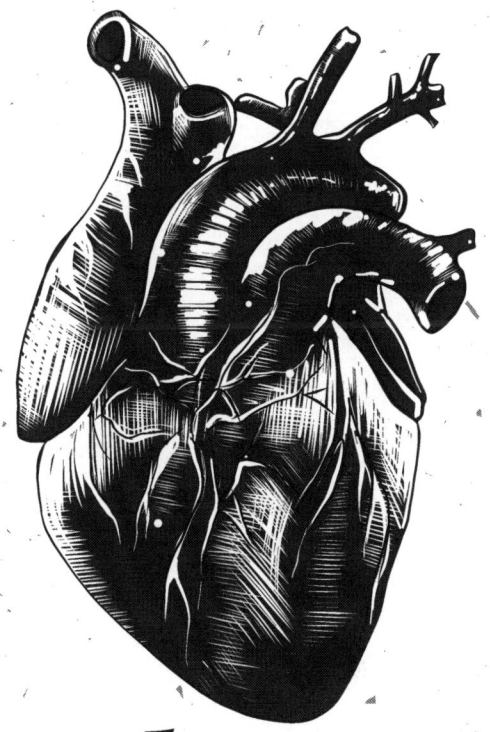

heart

even when the beat is broken
you always dance for me

1122

when you look into your eyes
who do you see?

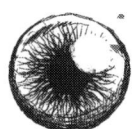

TO CHASE YOURSELF;
IN MIRRORS.
IN PEOPLE
IN DREAMS
IN THOUGHTS,
IN LIFE

**WHEN ALL ALONG
YOU WERE RIGHT HERE**

Don't let their approval be
the only key
to the doorway of your daylight.
For you see darling,
you've got so much magic in those fingertips
and pretty words inside that mind,
but do it all a great injustice
when you leave yourself behind.
If you keep waiting for the green light,
or someone else to take the lead,
you'll carry 'round unsettled feelings
of a girl scared to be seen.

I've felt
my time slip
through your fingers
as I floated
on the idea of us

...

now there you sit
                    debating me

& while I wait,
can't help but think
how many seconds spent loving you
might just have gone to better use
if I had chose to chase me instead.

what if I met a soul mate

or what if I just had fun

what is it I'm looking for

before I turn and run

heart beats & rates increasing

new bed to lease love to

tangled in & through another...

but am I the seeker

or the lover?

I don't blame you
for all the ways
I cut myself short
for all the space in my mind
you take occupancy
for all the questions I'm seeking
answers to
when others are waiting
longer in queue

I don't hate you
for the ways you
soak up my mind
and fill my heart
spinning circles of a pit within me
leaving my mind a dizzy haze

you're just this kind of ecstasy
a high I can't quiet explain
but while you set my skin on fire
I can't help but feel the flames

you're right there
in arms reach,
my eyes focused on you

we side step
burnt bridges
that torched territories new

hands shaking
heart racing
we keep waiting for the sun

but as I gain on you
I'm gathering
that I should fold and run

Is it to you
or from you?
don't leave yet, can't see through...

another day I'll wait for you
but leave you more
each time I do

KMN

I speak to the beat that's always led me

I want to love you the way I loved them.

I want to hold you tight, draw you in

erase your worries and paint your sorrows gold.

I want to dress you up, take you out

spin you around 'til we grow old.

I want to take your broken pieces,

fold them into something new.

I want to get you drunk on daylight,

reflect your magic back to you.

I want to show you how you dazzle,

I want to show you all your truth

That my love is not a daydream,

it's been waiting here for you.

instead of trying

to feel safe

**you should try
to feel free**

Lay me down slowly
as the beat carries our souls away
to clouds floating like ships lost at sea
with no one left in the world
but you and me
in your eyes I find the line of in-between
    of what life is
        & what it could be.

no matter the tangle
of fates and sheets
our hearts are marked
in winding streets
soul location
where we breathe
a matter of time
to melt into me
tongues left untied
we'll start something new
heart beating patterns
already tied to

all the love that I seek
all the values I bleed
all the strength that I need
all the air that I breathe

all approval I chase
all these dreams that I race
all the beauty I face
all the trust that I trace

is already within

elements

from the sky we came
from the earth we rise
from the fire we feel
from the sea we heal

[144]

SLEEP IN THE STARS
DREAM IN THE SKIES

& NEVER LOSE SIGHT
OF HOW INFINITE YOU ARE
AND THE MIRACLE THIS ALL IS

It was both a power
      and a curse
to feel every wave
      so deeply in the blood

fuel your passions
like wild fire
but beware the burn
of heavy flame

keep it tame
with steams of feeling
& thoughts left cleared
of any name

rise from ash
to cleanse your sorrows
soon your feet
find ground and then

strike a match
against tomorrow
set it all ablaze again

KMN

find your equilibrium

I drift away from you
to skies of navy blues
find clouds to cry into
fresh seas to bathe me new

run fields of thick lush greens
new world where I am seen
I glow in evergreen
heart free to
        new bloodstreams

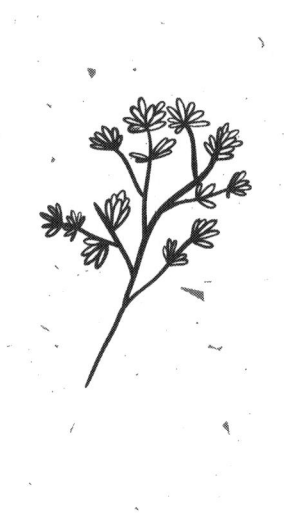

the bordering line
                between earth and the sky,

melted fire and ice
                that danced in your eyes.

a shooting star
free flamed desire
the earthly one became

with feet to dirt
long legs in skirts
hair tangled and untamed

walls built too high
to drown the cries
trap doors to depths left banned

clear curtain rests
a ghostly touch
no home to call her land

seas diving deep
a meeting match
heart closing like clenched fist

in icy depths
gasping for air
she breaks through earths surface

sky high she sits
above the clouds
her world awaits below

the wheels of fate
spin round again
the only truth she knows

KMN

stand
swim

burn
breathe

Next time
  I let mirrors
    show me my reflection
I will know how much smoke
    viels the eyes that aren't mine.

snow

it sprinkles down the town
around you
and chills the world fresh
and new

162

DON'T FEAR THE NIGHT,
OR THE WINTER FOR IT'S TRUTH
OF CAST SHADOWS AND COLD BREEZE

TURN ON YOUR LIGHT
BURN YOUR INNER FIRE
LET SNOW BRING CALM AND EASE

She was born a winter girl,
heart covered in ice.
As the snow fell around her,
came sharp eyes to entice.
A lone wolf to harsh weather,
sharp teeth and cold sheets.
At full moon he curled 'round her
thawed away

her deceits

first snow fall 2018 //

I'm looking out of my window;
the sky is that particular shade of navy blue
fading into fresh icy hues
that tend to fill a winter night sky.

a white blanket casts the ground beneath me
reflecting the same shine that glitters
from the stars above.

without a trace of movement outside
it's like time is standing still
I feel a fraction of infinity
right here in this moment

and the warmth that fills me
is a feeling I hope you'll find
in your life many times
a magic so simple

the same journal post turned poem

a warm buzz of the skin
as eyes race white drift skies
out a cool glass window
reflecting stars in my eyes

no trace of movement
time freezing the grounds
a heart burning warm
winter nights being found

KMN

blame it on our
mercury//

like a chilling mystery came the dawn of new light
asleep; sets of eyes I pretend could be mine
truths shed the seas between me and you
waging war; fight or flight leaving this love in ruin

I want to write you into winter

I want to rip you seam to seam

I want to tape us back together

I want to find a page to scream

I want to fold you like a love note

I want to leave the ink unseen

I want to trace my way back to you

I want to tell you everything

it falls around like icy dust

from pages written long ago

we danced away in tiny globes

our stories still left so untold

white blankets drape like times before
across the lands from peak to shore
in secret stars and shimmering lights
she laid her head to rest that night

and in her sleep, she found a door

to a world built just for her

should your days lose their rays
or the world steal your throne

let me walk through your maze
come and steal your alone

to see

the lift of your shoulders

the soft dance of your feet

your smile growing bolder

mix-match sins grin defeat

your dancing doll;

I twirl around you

our hands up high,

thoughts down low

but I blink and

you're another

you think of me come winter snow

tucked away in a corner
I watched the snow fall outside my window
as if nothing had changed
since the last icy season
the city painting itself with white icing
from an early full moon
and to my truths I note
that there are few things we know constant
in a life so ever-changing...

but big cities and ocean coasts
however different,
would always have seasons
which would leave souls with no exception
to such a constant rule

looking out another window
to the first fall of a new winters snow,
I knew;

no matter how much a girl loved
the warmth of a summer sun,
the whispers of winters
always brought her heart to new truths

sun

daylight igniting a light within
eyes closed
head back
  I drink her in

LEAN BACK
OPEN UP
AND STOP
ALL THAT HIDING

I put out my fires
I forfeit my fight
Spreading new wings now
Fresh air I take flight

KMN

Wake up
Stand up.
Take a deep breath.
Take it all in.

This is it.
This is what you've been waiting for.

I want you to shine louder than the
screams stolen from you in your sleep

KMN

SUNNY AFTERNOONS
FT. THOUGHTS OF YOU

I'll let the sun,
Pour over me.
I'll see new heights.
I'll plant new seeds.
Grow and glow,
A beat or two.
I'll breathe a bit,
I'll wait for you.

I hope that even as the light fades on the world around you

And you begin to feel the cold pinch your cheeks

That you find peace in the friendly face of the never changing sun

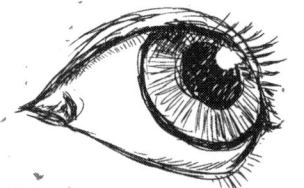

clocks locked
keys made cut to
black holes colliding
in layers of the in between

a sacred place
where we can meet

NO MATTER
WHAT FILLS
YOUR
DAYLIGHT
HOURS...

No matter what you
call your "norm"
given this chapter of
your life, no matter
the unfinished
thoughts you can't
seem to shake from
your mind; smile.

Life, however rich
and random it may
be, does not need to
be so serious.

The light you see in others

is shining down on you too.

no matter the season

you're sitting in

if the weather has called

for heavy cloud and rain

find peace in declaring

a spring season

to your souls slumber;

see what the darkness gave light to,

bring to life that dreamy state of wonder,

plant fresh ideas is the soft earth below,

and rise with the part of you that's ready to

feel free and new.

I hope you choose to see daylight
to burn with an inner sun.

I know the night can get dark
and the ride confusing,
but lift your face to the light,
melt your shoulders away
and drink a breath deep

There's a fire inside of you.
find it.
fuel it.

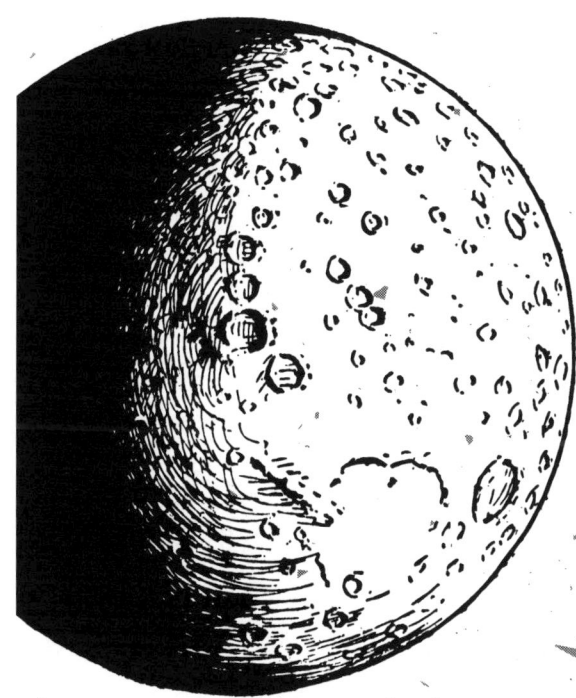

moon

she sees me in my darkest hour
she knows just who I am
she calls to me
delicate flower
let your power be your friend

|208|

WHEN I RUN FROM MY DARKNESS
I RUN FROM MY LIGHT TOO

NO LONGER FEARING DEATH
I BEGAN TO FEEL ALIVE.

UNDER THE LIGHT OF THE MOON

mourn the loss
of all that you once were
to make room in your soul
for all you are to become.

I know these heavy thoughts
are merely just feelings
& I've found that in their release
I free myself

for what once bound my feet
laced my back to new wings

KMN

let go of the grip
you hold so tightly
to the world
for every little thing
is going to be okay

KMN

love letters to

the moon;

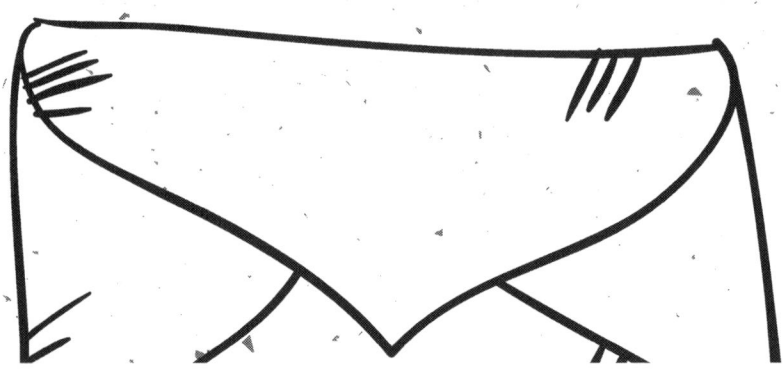

12:14am

you've followed me
through towns and cities
years and lifetimes

faces fading in and out
painting shades in patterns
guiding me home to the soul
that rests deep inside

orbiting around the idea
that all we've ever sought
and we ever seek
is and always has been

        orbiting within

bring forth all the sides

of the life you create

bleed them of their darkness

surrender the divine

recharge under the moonlight

and then explode again

for after all

you are only stardust

cycling and shining

your whole light through.

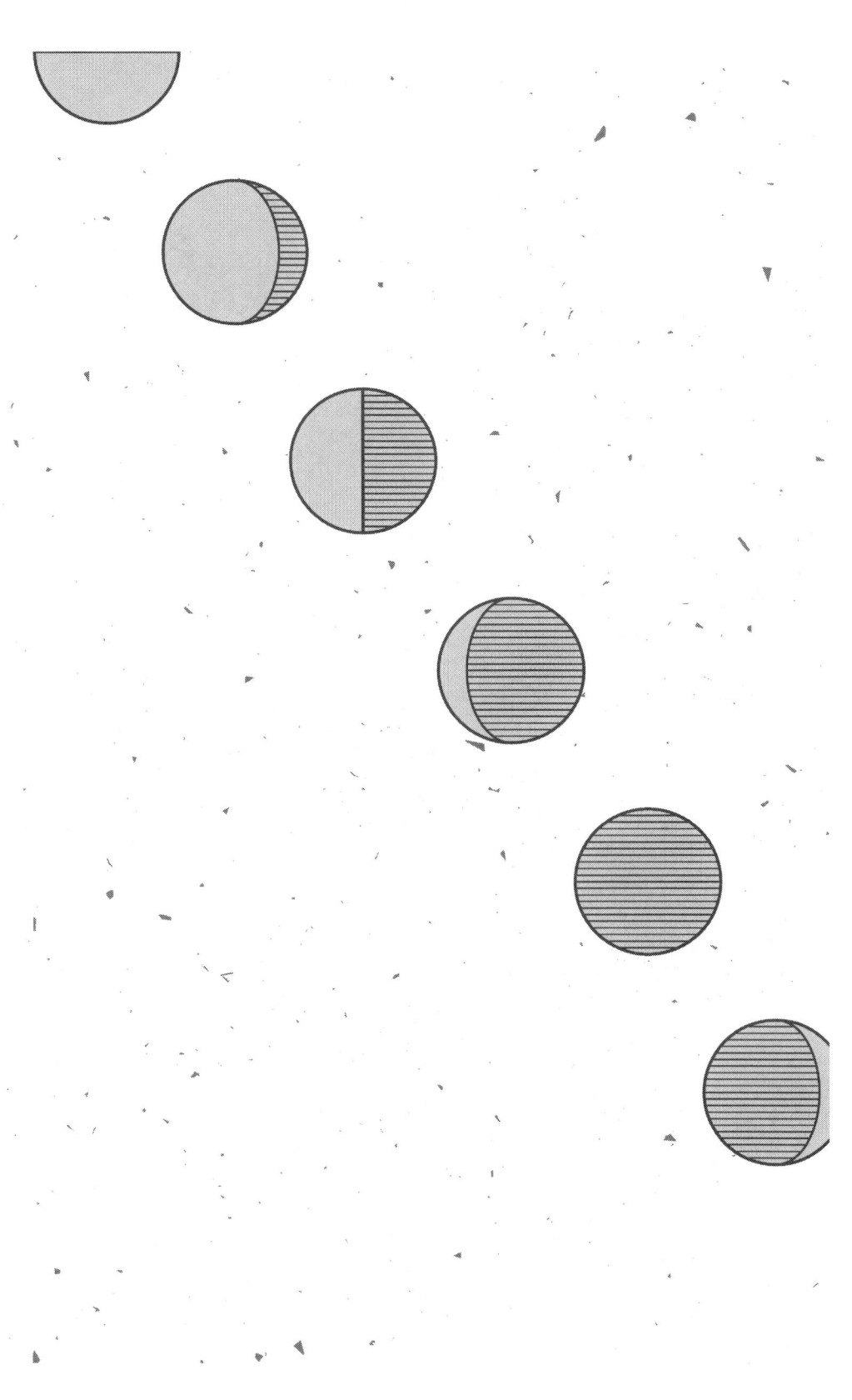

LEARN TO LOVE YOUR SHADOWS
FIND PEACE IN YOUR DARK NIGHTS
IT'S NOT ABOUT THE FIGHT OR BATTLE
BUT A CHANCE TO SHINE
YOUR LIGHT

TIME-OUTS TO TAKE, THEY'LL GIVE YOU
LAY LOW, LET YOUR FIRE COOL
THE ENERGIES YOU'LL GAIN HERE
REFILLING EVERY POOL

sometimes it burns
to willingly paint days
with missing you

when I could be drawing
someone new.

Retreat to your centre,

not your sadness.

I'm no longer new

to the new moons late hour

when the world gets most dark

I stopped desperately searching

for a light in the night

and instead turned to

the guidance of my own.

it's easier
to look through the mirror
then at it.

it's not about what you're
seeng
it's about how you're seeng it.

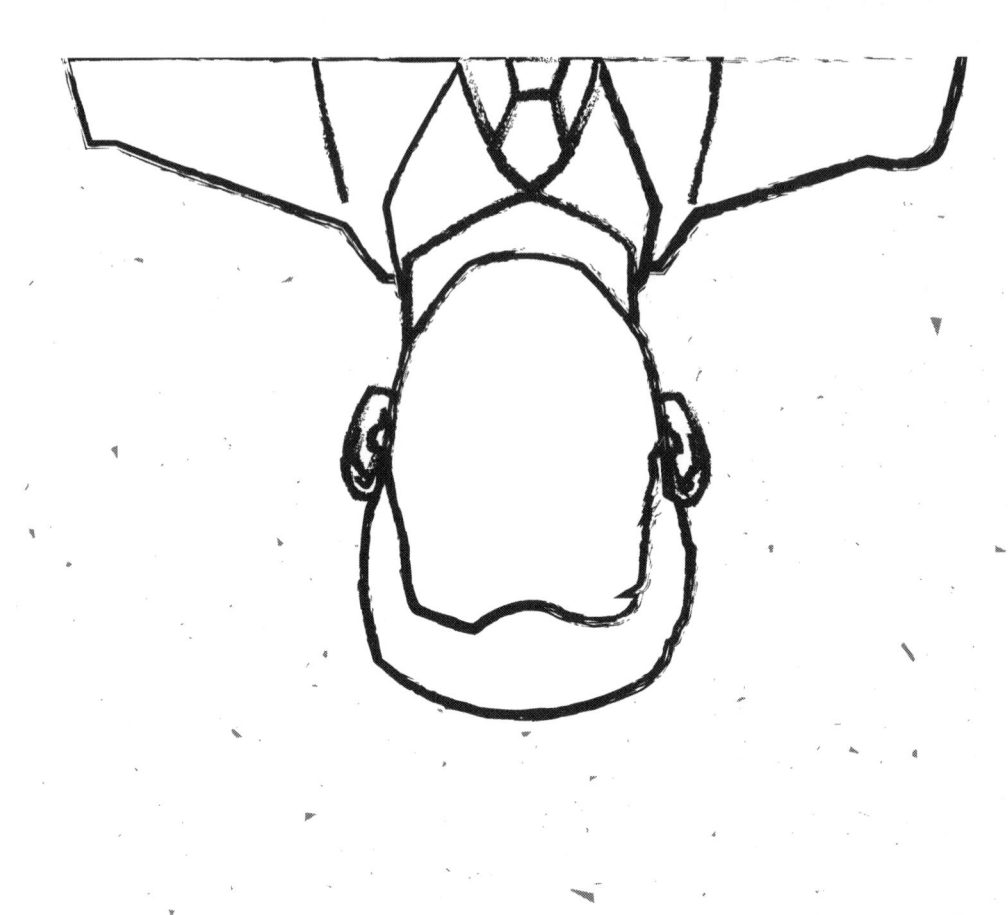

wild, puzzling,
passionate and mad
with a doubtful reputation
and such youthful disposition

my name
his willow to wither
with rich empty talk
bloviate by the winds of luck
or rather - a legacy to make

eyes like drawn windows
taking intoxicated blows
winking till I wipe out
destroying me with one last drink

and the whispers of bystanders
pulling wires and setting plans
of new suitors to defeat
all these manipulating measures

air

the space inbetween
every sound, every thing
every being.

I LAY BACK IN THE SPACE BETWEEN BEACH AND SUN—
LIKE A BLANKET OF SILK SUNLIGHT POURS
ACROSS WARM COLLAR BONES

I LET THE WARMTH BEAM INTO MY BEING
LIGHT FILTERING THROUGH PALMS
THE UNIVERSE WAVING WITH THE OCEAN

I WONDER WHAT MIGHT WAIT IN SUCH FRESH AIR.

Is it really love?
Or are am I just another name
To add to your list
Of pretty little things?

You'll run cobblestone streets,
taste caramel gelato and fly clouds
far away from here.

When you do I hope you'll see
scenes that make you so serene
that you just might think of me.

I hope you'll smile on the play
of an imaginary scene where our
souls stayed marked in matching
coordinates.

And you'll still dream of me in other
worlds where there wasn't so much
growing still left to do.

KMN

we danced in the laughter

of what it was like to burn alive

our monsters riding shotgun

we drank the sun

we let them drive

stars danced across our eyes

as the sea tore itself wild

you turned your head and promsied me

forever young despite the miles.

your fires could not burn
and your lands would never be
without all the sacred space
of cherished air in between

I feel it in the freeze
short circuits
left dazed and confused
in the chaos of your masking
goodbyes I never told you
you never gave the chance to
waiting on words that blind me
while you look the other way
killing slow the only source
that ever gave you air to breathe
and space to be

waiting for your light to cast

around our fading shadows;

a silver lining that never came

stay exactly as you are

your soul makes me
believe in magic;

you carried me
bright and high
painted purple
and burning blue

safe and loved
souls in circles
poised and proud
came lovers new

fire

mirrored signs' burn alive
drowning out the dying
'flames'

the weight of you
lifts from my shoulders
tight grip relaxing
into waves drifting
in and out
of knowing you
you could be it all
or sweet nothing

only time will tell...
thought I might see you there

KMN

I see your face
in passing strangers

the only ghost
I like to see

KMN

WHAT WOULD IT MEAN
not to love you?
WHAT WOULD IT BE LIKE
to put this fire out?

what if I stopped believing

his eyes seem deeper
his touch more electric
his soul shined
more golden than the rest?
what if he was just another
hand that held mine
heart that marked time
safe corner I tucked into
for a little while
however fleeting...

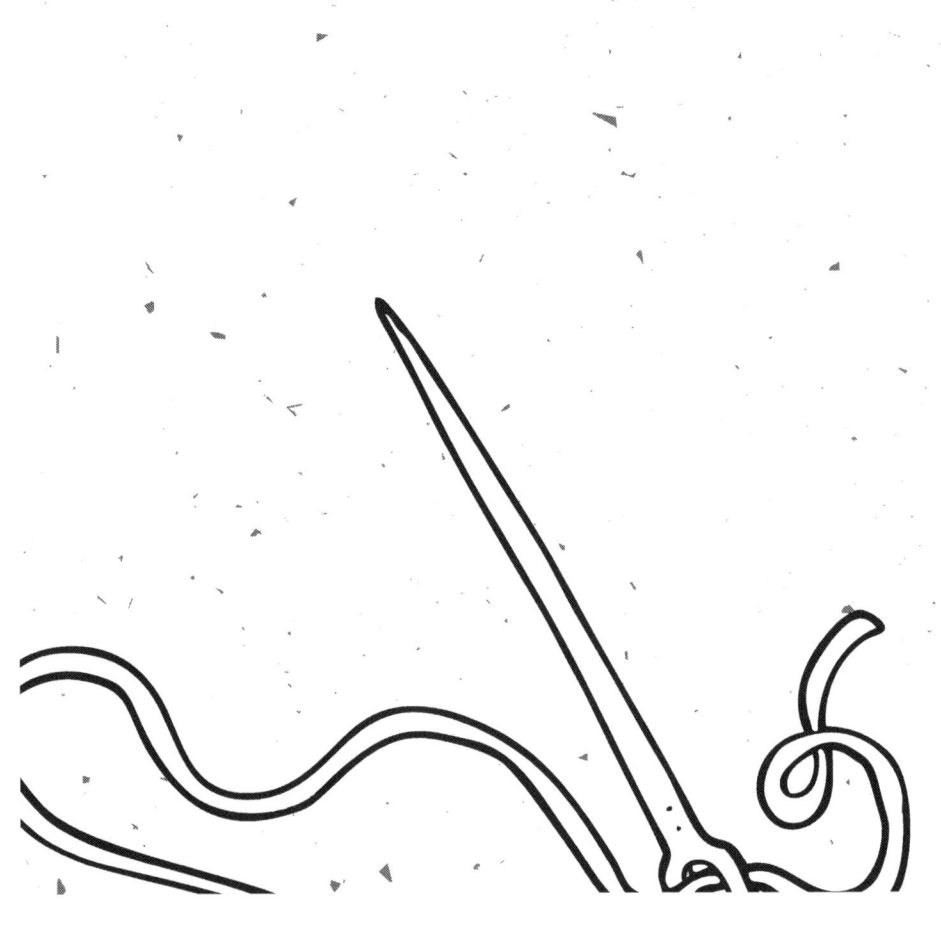

CAN'T PIN an outcome
YOU DOWN I can't control
CAN'T DREAM a thought
YOU UP I can't let go
CAN'T WORK making time
YOU OUT pass ever slow
CAN'T WISH a thread to life
YOU IN I trust to sow

I'm almost certain
there are times
the clock struck 11:11

and I wished for you
without knowing it.

he locks his eyes
a new demise

she sways her hips
to someone new

unsure what to think
try not to at all
weight like cement
your name the brick wall

fates cruelest trick
of tempt when you came
we're not the other's
can't win if it's games

this hold you have on me
see it broken in the mirror
write our rules out in the blood
head and heart keep making deals

clustered thoughts stuck swirling
my sad eyes growing tired
no time left to wait here
your secret unadmired

I stare out a new high rise
sunlight flickering through trees
put you down a thousandth time

go home...
new thoughts of you breathe

the clock strikes midnight.
  on another year I should be kissing you.

unstitch your heart
you keep far away
new trick up your sleeeve
tiring games to play

run from yourself now
my turn for dismay
predicted this leaving
safe fears if we stayed

tip toe to our towers
metanoia our days
wallflower our wrecking
time painting new greys

earth

plant your seeds with the right intentions
water them with love and watch as the
earth breathes all you dream to life

I HAD TO TEACH MYSELF TO ROOT
THE WAY A TREE DOES
TO THE GROUND..
I HAD TO MELT THE PINS AND PRICKS
OF FEAR AND FILL MY FEET WITH
SAND; WEATHERING STORMS THAT
CAME FROM TWISTING LOOSE THE
CANISTER I KEPT AIR TIGHT INSIDE.
AND WHEN LIGHTNING STRUCK
IT LIGHT UP THE SKY
LEAVING ME STARING THIRD EYE
DEEP INTO THIS SEA OF MINE.

TO FIND THE STRENGTH
TO BREATHE AGAIN,
I STEPPED BACK AND TOOK THE TIME
TO ROOT MY HEART TO THE DIVINE.

a champagne pop of young heartbeats,
lacing laughs to tangled sheets.
you're solid earth
you let me lean
new city boy, too good to me

year one
bled in
read

but then he rose to become
more...

the sculptor in
dawning
back to his clay with yearning eyes
ready for a new beginning

only to take off unfinished
never done
his hands still cast in plater
leaving behind the astonishing piece
of half-hearted lessons
left for me to learn

KMN

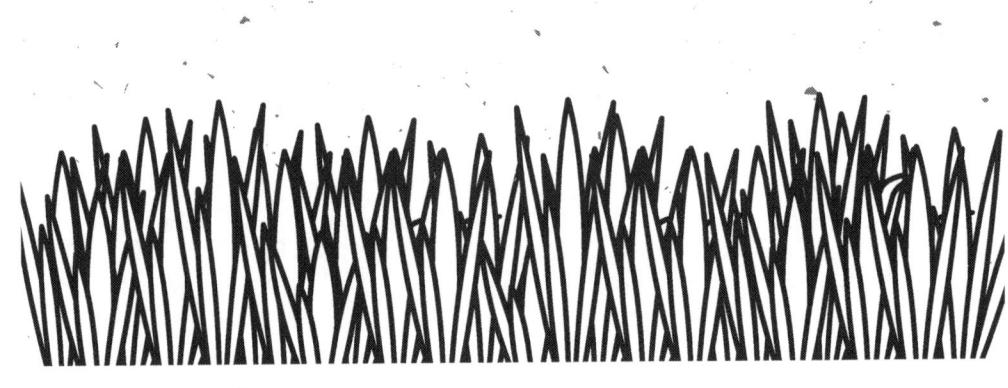

bones to grass, eyes to skies

we fall back into the clouds

& dream of places we'd like to

drift on rays of painted sun

crossed fingers signing deals

to trace thoughts from the air

burning them through flame

and bathing them in care

to grow new lands fertilized

by our deepest desires.

sometimes I miss the things
that pained me most
for the times they felt like home;
& while I'm good at wrapping myself into
a place to rest and nest that's new
it makes me nostalgic for homes
that were once no good for me

I stared down the long road of what I knew waited
I felt the fog lift, the heat shift;
a soul switching gears.

taking off from all that burned me
blindfolded and bewildered
ready for something new.

the world always seemed to look better from up here

but with tired eyes I could see

truths growing unclear

the air that held me

with so much space to breathe

choked me back down

to solid ground

root
yourself:

in the people you love,

in the things you tune into,

in the breath you're now taking,

in the thoughts you are making,

sink yourself deep into a steady state of seeing.

i made my world so small

when I let it revolve around you

A subtle shift of make belief
you can dream and draft
anything you need
just plant it like a seed

and boy, how it grows.

water

the deeper you go
the deeper it gets
until all that you feel
is all that is left

1298|

paint me a picture of all the things
that keep you up at night

HE'S A WORK OF ART
PAINTED WITH THE KIND OF SOUL
YOU WANT TO WATCH

FILL A CANVAS

Clouds coloured like lead
Love burning hot, red
Hands trace along skin
City lights growing dim
Lips melt into waves
Lost fates being saved
Tidal waves to and from
Souls melt, veins go numb
Time freezes, world stops turning
Silent words whisper yearning
Silhouettes dance the dark
Crossing x's over hearts
Tucked away above streets
A rhythm syncing two heartbeats

16.09

with seas so deep
who could ever swim?

who could stand in the tides,
resist the rushing waves
of two souls cracked so wide open?

KMN

Damp hair

Cool skin

Late afternoon Grey

Your eyes

Draw lines

Where fingertips play

The chords

Dance freely

The room starts to sway

Lost tides

Finding shore

As they collide and drift away.

Is this me

or a reflection

of who I think I should be?

A trace of free

in wrong directions

I chased my way to the sea.

KMN

I read back on the way my skin used to crawl
and burn with the questions I let go unanswered for so long.
My days inching in ways that never felt so right in being so wrong.

I kept waiting for the moments to snap to life in the way I
had envisioned.
Learning to grow and glow in ways that felt more fluid.
But I should have known by how it was written in every action
despite the contrast of every word.

It was my choice to look in other directions.
but with everything so easily tied to things I wished to share
how could I ever just let go?

My biggest fear always being that it wouldn't be enough

but I cut you the grace anyways in case of hold out;

trying to communicate in languages we don't speak.

It's hard to share what you know when you sense everything you say

being broken down into rights and wrongs.

Filtered perspectives you try to understand but realze have nothing to do with you.

The entire lesson being nothing of them and all within the letting go;

No longer holding back in restraint, afraid of drowning in waters so deep

without arms there to catch me.

Knowing the pain and disappointment written in our contract

I still act like it's nothing new, becuase I tell myself the others

don't hit the way you do.

But the only truth that tested true was eyes that held better than the rest

Everything else; another lessons for the damsel

saving herself the distress.

I breathe you in
translucent vapour
you sink your way into my sleep

**I drop my guard
you drop your anchor
open seas we take the leap.**

I lay there, ice water pinning my back to the depths below

And on shore, the eyes of most everyone I know

In waiting they watch if I might sink below

Stare up in straight focus to nothing but grey skies

As I feel my world shrink, it expands in true size

And just as I sink, I feel new life rise

I'm not sure if I'm one to say I know much about love
But with you it feels like I wrote it before I ever read it.
And it keeps your pages open like a bookmark in my mind.
So I keep reaching, keep wondering
keep trying to write you down and breathe you in.
as if I already feel it written, like every tattoo on my skin.

Like a masterpiece of technicolour,
hand painted just for me.
He was beautiful, but not just in
the way that he looked...

he was beautiful for the life behind those eyes
and the stories they told
the depths they hold, from lifetimes long before our own
for his old soul with young energy
his cool stance, his hot hands
for the way he wrote my name in the dark
his beauty lies deeper than the surface of what is
it sows stories of what once was and what will be
despite the noise of our days and the chaos of our minds
there's something laced in rich gold that
thread a path from him to me
and every time I get around him,
it's the only colour I want see
sometimes so rich it scares me
for he doesn't hold me like a damsel, distressed and weak
but drinks me in like effervescent energy;
a safe place to lean
no matter where I run to or who's body warms my sheets
his beauty has a way of finding me in my dreams
so I take down all the frames of hearts I loved before
I sweep up their broken pieces like pixie dust off the floor
with a bare room, a blank canvas and a vision in my mind
I make way for the art that's about to paint my life
for the pockets of light and laughter
we couldn't see but somehow knew
and the souls that will come after
once we age a love that's new
but this time, I won't get lost in the brush strokes
that stop and start
for in the centre of this masterpiece,
I didn't hang his heart;

This time,
I painted my own
gold and dazzling,
just as he is.

fates

could you believe
that there might be
energy already tied
to your own

1320

I set free the three words
                choking me
            your name giving their weight
                new meaning

show me all the ways
you burn for fear

think your damaged goods but baby
you're only afraid
like the rest of us

now you see me, now you don't
say we're leaving, know we won't
met at midnight, chased the sun

star crossed lovers come undone

it was evening as I reached

little lies in the middle

awaiting my one

lion-like and curious

with eyes like glass

rapidly making a name

of himself

& delight that it might be you

his place of safe and light

though you might talk it over

occasional questions of interjection

he tilts his head with honest eyes

His theory; the little lies you foretold

becoming true.

words fall down onto me
perched on the edge of here
& somewhere else entirely
anchored by the weight of your bones
to the depths of your soul
we swim in iris pools
wondering what damage
we could do

KMN

when my mind's eye wanders to you

I look up to see you turning pages

just like the ones we write now

and as I wake

I race to see you

but you're never really there

and perhaps you never will be.

I ran away to lands of ice
where castles carved the mountain sides
and air painted rainbows
standing beneath all that was left of me
a misfit soul with layers chopped away
me eyes lit a blue fire
as I watched the hourglass flip new.

KMN

are fates sealed by hand to pen
pen to paper...

or is the ink already written?

whisper me secrets

no one else knows

cross me your fingers

leave our fates unknown

match me in lost bets

where did we go?

trace back our first steps

follow me home.

One day I'm going to look over to the couch
and see you sitting there bathed in morning glow.
As you read your lastest, scents of old paper will
fill the air and hold our rested eyes
My gaze will wisp with the steam swirls
from coffee that touches your lips
I'll feel your fingers down the spine
of the pages you drink in
I'll use our smiles like ink for new stories we
stumble through, drunk on nothing but the notion
that we finally made it to where
we were always meant to be.

chaos

lost in the shadows
of everything that never was
but I feared into fruition

342

IT TAKES A TOLL ON THE SOUL
TO WORK OUT SUCH
POWERFUL KNOTS;
WITH WOUNDS TO NURSE
BROKEN BONES TO HEAL
HOW COULD ONE EXPECT
TO DO SO WITHOUT SHEDDING
A TEAR OR TWO?

I kept building windows
to watch the world pass by
faces soaking in the daylight
while I'm tucked away inside
I wondered with my silhouette
why I always had to hide
glass reflecting my minds eye
of all the pretty pannelled lies
I built to rid myself from trying

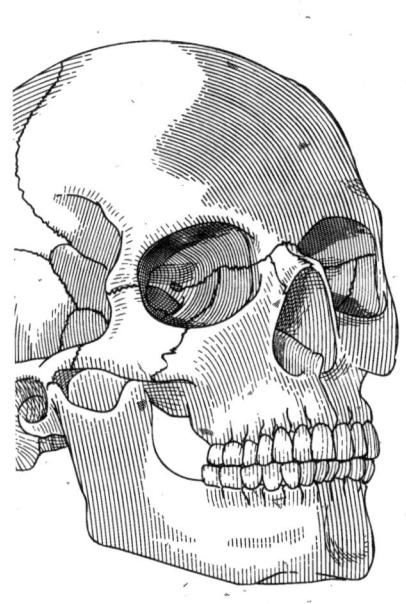

Each night I drowned my veins
I couldn't help but sit
in the morning thought;
& perhaps I was
thinking too deeply
but...

is there ever really
a right way
to balance poison in the
blood?

how can you expect to live
a life so full and free
with an empty stomach
& bones as thin as thieves?

KMN

thrashing against waves that pull deep
to the tides of rivalling beliefs
of what it is to just be
dark currents masking
tiny islands of desire
that feel like home for just a while
before nightfalls and you're left
with nothing but monsters in the eyes
of those you thought kindest
you jump back into the sea
of sensations you sink deep
to find your footing in the chaos
of all lies above shore
and only when you lose the air
that was keeping you alive
do you drink the messages weighing you down
unknotting your spirit afloat
to find new skies so blue
you only notice them for the contrast
to what was once
such bittersweet greys

All these numbers never adding up

to the proper measurements of love

I kept depriving myself of with each shrinking digit.

What am I doing?

   Why am I doing this?

But worst of all,

     why does it sometimes feel so nice

to make home in the shadows

growing under my eyes?

When all I wanted was light

I only gave myself dark.

When all I needed was love

I sank their hate in my heart.

When I wanted nothing more than to build the strength of a

thousand lions; pouring any pain into a wild roar...

I shrank myself away

to the size of a mouse

& then wondered why the world

felt so cold.

KMN

It boils over,

burning away at all the soft edges

of beautifully living

and free.

The chaos cutting away the oxygen

from silent elephants

that fill the room.

To feel you;

pouring out of my eyes

bleeding into my words like venom.

Tracing your fingers down my spine with claws so deep

I'm afraid for just a moment that my armour

is the same weak skin you once turned ghost

When you stole the gravity

that held my spirit with each gulp

you guilted from me

And now that I'm free

I catch your shadow in the hearts around me

you're still haunting.

I stare it down
with dares
of sharp claws
and bared teeth

but from my mind
I created you
so I can bleed you dry
just the same

while you grasp at my feet
threatening to eat
me whole
my eyes take aim
about to dive
in freesol

rain

heart splits like the clouds
that came to wash it all away

I LET YOU GO
I WATCH YOU LEAVE
EVEN THOUGH YOUR SOUL SHINES GOLD
AND OUR MINDS SPEAKS DISCREET;
WE WERE FLOATING ON CLOUDS
SURFING TO A SWEET BEAT

WHEN I FINALLY REALIZED
YOUR MELODY WASN'T ME

AN ODD FEELING TO MOURN

souls gone but still living

chest growing heavy
from the space between
the person you were
and who you came to be

pain pinning
eyes sinking
hands shaking
guilt gaining

at the idea that it could ever mean
too much for you
to be more for me

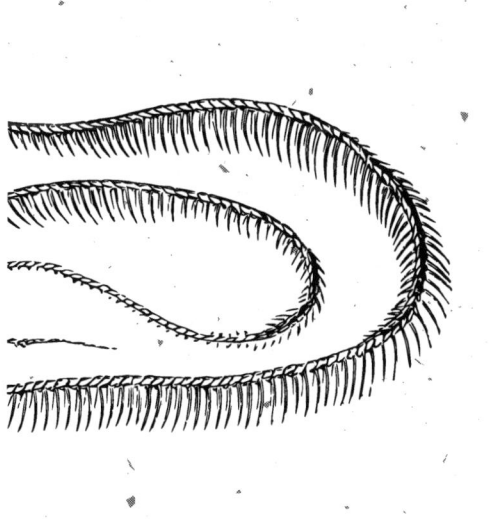

I think back to the suns setting
golden hour painted by young hearts

there was me
& then there was you

cold temperatures filling the room
a dizzy haze of ice capped mountains
& deep truths
passed between two

volcanoes catch stars
that blanketed sea foam skies
tucking hearts to bed that watched
the hour turn 2:00

in snow sparkling white
& waters burning blue
the girl within me
loved the boy that was you

KMN

minor chapters

that felt like the whole story

scare me into thinking

that I might not know love at all

our waves caught

tides pulling us deep
our souls made of the same thing
sinking slowly in the overflow

but too much water
left no air to breathe.

why is it always the best hearts

crying tears over the worst ones?

U

4

•

I

5

•

I

8

I've loved you with a peaceful, force that has carried me far along this road with you.
From the way you walked to the way you said my name, you had me pinned with a magnetic
force I never questioned but simply enjoyed.

You somehow found a way to melt years of ice I didn't see surrounding me;
As I watch it play back now, I know I wouldn't change a thing.
I would still walk down those stairs and into your car. I would still order that glass of
chardonnay while a piano played away my hopes that you might just lean in and kiss me.
I'd still curl up in your sweater after flying home from sunshine state; watching
midnight streetlights change from red to green when I realized with a sudden certainty
that I was falling for you. I would still wake you up in the middle of the night, the
croaks of cottage frogs filling the air as I told you that I loved you.
My feet would carry me across all the dance floors and sidewalks and my lips would still
play with your name, scripting memories I pray I'll never forget.

But it seems as though we're at our turning point. I didn't want to call the battle,
because the only thing harder than picturing a life where we found a way to meet in the
middle is a life where you're not standing there at all.

But I'll always want open windows where you wish you had closed blinds.
You'll sigh at my movements in the early hours of the day and I'll roll my eyes in
frustration each time you ask me to come out your way.

I pray that your life is full of love and joy;
that maybe somewhere down the line we might cross paths and smile –
understanding then all the lessons we're learning now.
Until then, know no matter how far our souls grow, your name will always bring
a warm smile to my face.

YOU'LL SPEND A LIFETIME
WAITING TO FEEL BETTER
IF YOU KEEP PUTTING OFF
ALL THE THINGS
YOU KNOW WILL
MAKE YOU FEEL BETTER

Do you ever wake up
in the middle of the night
without all the bright lights
and daily distractions
find peace in truths
you've been searching for
all daylight?

TEN FIVE
TWENTY
EIGHTEEN

even the seas capsize
with every heart beat of mine
that beats loudly in time
it calms slow a sweet divine
of what it is to feel your shine
broken up by dark skies
and storms that drain
from my eyes.

sinking deep
strong tides
"I'm over it"
I lie.

IT
DIDN'T
END
VIOLENT

There was no blood spilt
Instead, it fizzled,
days sizzling slowly,
until the spark disappeared.
And the veil fell,
showing me what was
really behind.
Just another mirror,
tied to a root to find
the knots to untangle
my heart for someone new.

lightning

just as the storms hit and it
feels like you may drown
light strikes the sky bringing to
life all you couldnt see in the dark

1384

DAZED AND DAZZLING

PIN YOUR DREAMS HIGH

FIND THE MAGIC

THAT'S YOURS TO CHASE

AND WHEN YOU FIND IT

DON'T THINK TWICE.

Girl in Calico

You'll know how far you've grown

when songs that once made you cry

make you dance.

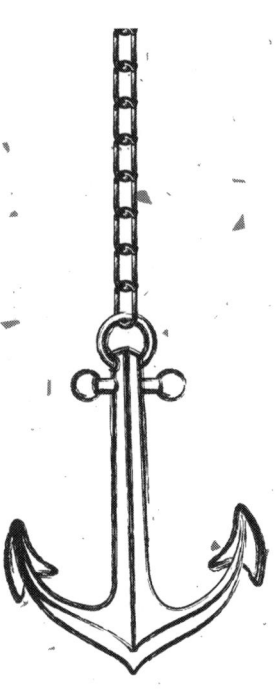

real change doesn't happen when
intentions are anchored
in shallow waters

to redirect a soul we must dive
into our deep unknown
and untie our minds eye
from the false safety of land

sometimes we may sink,
sometimes we may tire,
but building true kingdoms
has never been easy work

don't lose effectiveness
chasing efficiency.

to all the daughters //

It's okay to feel broken.
Don't run from it. Let it take you and teach you.

Instead of chasing perfection, embrace imperfection.
In chasing the illusion, you cut yourself off from all
the beauty in the chaos.

Travel light through life.
Keep only what you need and seek out laughter
when you feel heavy.

Being vulnerable doesn't make you weak.
It makes you strong.

If you're not real with yourself you'll stay stuck
running around your own house of mirrors.

Everyone has flaws.

Hiding from your responsibilities doesn't make them
go away.

Believe in your ability to accomplish whatever awaits
you.

It's never as bad as you think it's going to be.

People deserve a second chance...
but know your boundaries.
There are no such things as third and fourth
chances.

Just because you can doesn't always mean you
should.

Never underestimate the power of a solo Friday night
relaxing at home.

Happiness isn't a permanent state, but wholeness
and wellness can be.

If you have an opinion, it's best to back it up.

You already have enough.

You already are enough.

Ice cream is always a good idea.

So is a good jog.

Happy impulses are often fleeting.

Dance whenever the feeling arises.

Be open to saying yes.

Learn how to give a firm no.

Read and watch the classics. They're classics for a
reason.

No man is ever worth playing dumb.
If they can't handle your fire they don't get your
flame.

Don't let high school be the best years of your life.

Keep your man close but your best friends in the
same radius.

The only way out of something is to work your way
through it.

Self-esteem is just a self estimate. Don't aim low.

Trust your intuition.

Follow your gut.

Also follow your heart but take some common sense with you.

You are not all the horrible things you believe in your darkest hour.

Your past only defines you if you keep highlighting it.

You are so much more than your age, face and size.

Never let a day go by without listening to music.

The only wrong decision is not making one.

Be unapologetic.

Unless you mess up, then apologize and own your shit.

Take care of yourself.

Eat healthy food.

Go to bed early...

But know some of your best memories will be made the nights you stayed out late.

Fall in love with seeing the world.

Be yourself, especially when you're most afraid to.

Appreciate all the differences that create contrast in our world.

When a man shows you who he is, believe it.

You are the sun. You are the prize.

If it won't matter in 3 months or 3 years, it doesn't need to matter so much now.

Other women are your allies not your competition.

Comparing yourself is the fastest track to misery.

Jump in with all of your clothes on.

Jump in with all your clothes off.

Laugh as much as humanly possible.

Forgive the moment for not being what you hoped it would be, and then begin again.

Love and compassion are necessities not luxuries.

Never, ever underestimate yourself.

Unless you're drinking.

Know your worth.

Keep your head up.

Believe in magic.

Find confidence in being compassionate.

wear the
red
lipstick.

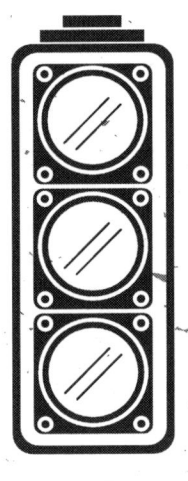

so you must decide;
who you'll be, what you want
the vision you see
see it, feel it, commit to it
believe in it without any proof

Why?

because unless you are fully
committed to who you are
and what you're here to do
the minute the moment arrives
you'll shrink back in worry and fear
killing all the opportunities to grow
into exactly who you were born to be

so you must decide;
will you dream bold
or will you settle in the questioning
of all that could have been
had you dared to chance yourself?

iphone
notes

hey siri↵
take note of my secrets
at three in the morning

where are you right now?

YOU MIGHT SAY AT YOUR DESK
IN AN OFFICE, YOUR BEDROOM
A CLASSROOM, A PARK, A BUS
WALKING DOWN THE STREET
OR OUT GRABBING A BITE TO EAT —
BUT ALL THOSE ANSWERS
WOULDN'T NECESSARILY BE TRUE...

WHERE WAS YOUR MIND A FEW MOMENTS
BEFORE YOU FOUND YOURSELF HERE?

YOUR BODY IS RIGHT HERE
READING THESE PAGES
BUT ON THE DAYS YOU MIGHT FIND
WORDS A LITTLE LESS ANCHORING
YOUR MIND IS USUALLY
SOMEWHERE ELSE ENTIRELY

WHERE WE FIND OUR THOUGHTS TO WANDER
ISN'T NECESSARILY UNIMPORTANT;
IT'S JUST THAT WHEN YOU
LOOK BACK ON YOUR LIFE
WHAT DO YOU WANT TO SEE?

THE THINGS YOU WERE THINKING ABOUT
OR THE THINGS YOU ACTUALLY DID?

Great things are coming.
Great things are already here.
Great things are happening.
Great things are all around you.

KMN

What game are
you playing?
And do you know
the rules?

There is no enemy.
Would you rather
be right or free?

your words say yes as

your eyes say no

your hands move in

but your body stays closed

lost in a madness I can't digest

loving you has always been such a sweet mess

KMN

while truth is important
perhaps it's not so much about
whether or not things are
actually real...

but whether
we believe them to be.

All teachings are the same:

To be happy you have to think positively.
To see things positively you need to be grateful.

let your why be stronger

than your need to know when

we are as interesting as what we

choose to do with our spare time

there is nothing for you to rush to discover

rather more of yourself for you to uncover

there is no easier path or better path

just different paths

only when you truly let go of all that is
not yours to know or have
can you finally take hold with both hands
all the magic that is yours to keep
ridding yourself the shadows
that have been hiding all your light
releasing the weight of elephants
that tricked you into believing
you could ever mean so little
with so much left to give,

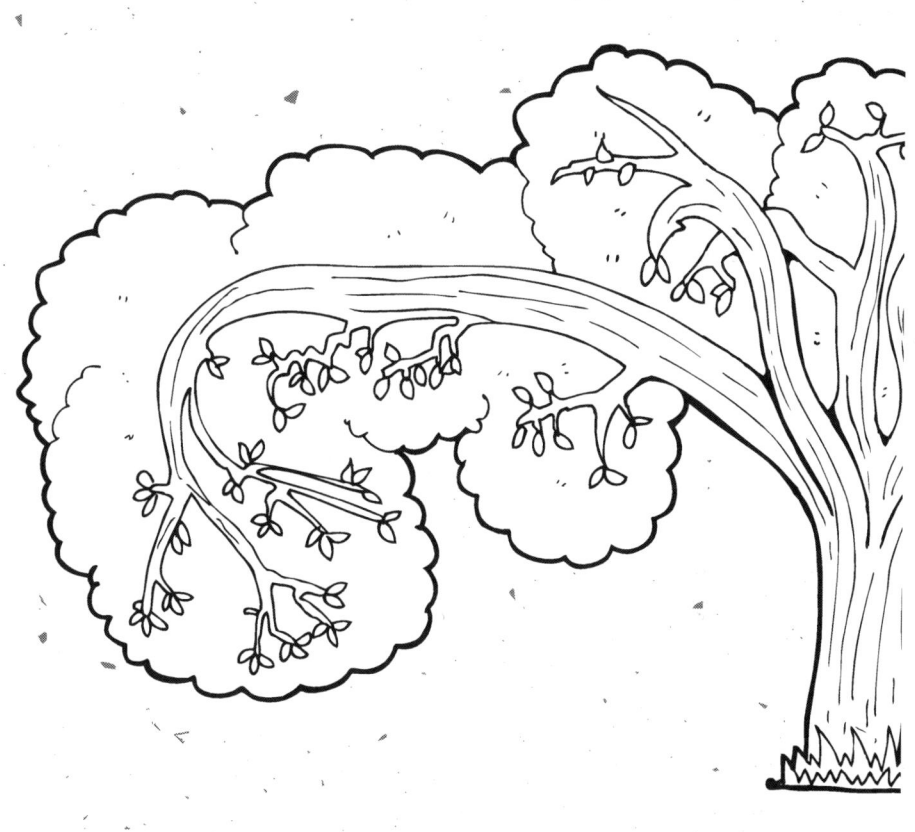

Made in the USA
San Bernardino, CA
10 April 2020